The Possibly Impossible Lives of
Charles 'Chuy' Chalmers
by Mic Fox

"On the chaotically-mild shores of America's jetski-
ridden north coast, an unknown author is approached
under bizarre circumstances to help ghostwrite the
memoirs of an eccentric older man. When the man's
stories begin to misfire, the author finds himself
caught between reality and the wild narratives we tell
ourselves about that reality."

To be read and or staged. If staged, 4-5 people along with improvised live music or a DJ will do.

Characters

```
1:Mic:     a Narrator. A writer. Husband to Molly.
2:Molly:   a Friend. Wife to Mic.
  Goosh:   a Flamboyant Queen of a Man. Husband to Chuy.
3:Sandy:   a Flamboyant Queen of a Woman. Wife to Chuy.
4:Chuy:    an Eccentric Old Mess of a Man. Husband to both
           Goosh and Sandy.
  Johnny:a Cuban pretending to be an Italian.
  Eddie:   a Biker who can't leave his past behind him
  Donnie:a Menace from another life.
  Chuck:   a Strange Old Mess of a Man. Twin brother of
           Chuy?
(The parts of Molly and Goosh can be done by two
  separate people. But why bother?)
```

Notes

Narration should be shredded at a rapid-fire pace, as to not bore the audience.

```
Dialogue should be treated conversationally and at a
whatever pace feels right.
```

The narrator, Mic, as well as the musicians, should feel free to break the 3rd wall when they see fit – for the benefit of the audience. Any little footnotes that you feel would add to the performance are more than welcome to be read aloud.

Because I am Mic. I may drift in and out of first/third person when writing notes and stage direction. I need you to work with me here. And hell, if you're reading this and planning on narrating, well then, you are he and you are me and we are all together. Eggman etc.

-When Mic's speaking to the audience as a Narrator, it's written like this.

```
-When Mic's speaking to other members of the cast, it's
  written like this.
```

```
[Sets may and should be moved around behind Mic
  narrating. If it's distracting, let it be funny.
  Obviously.]
```

All text and artwork Copyright 2025 by Mic Fox, Famly LLC
ISBN: 979-8-9934299-0-8

[Stage opens black. The sound of steel drum music, bar chatter, and motorcycles fades in. Music crescendos and becomes chaotic then drops, cuing a spotlight on a large plywood photo-op sign that you'd stick your head through at some vacation-style restaurant, making your body appear that it is a manatee. Sign reads, "Go Shuck Yourself! I'm at Sandy's."]

Mic   [On the phone, walking from off-stage]

I know I know. You don't think I know how wild this is? …

I don't know … I'm somewhere outside of Sandusky I think.

Yeah … I know … I mean … I guess I *feel* safe. It's just a weird parrot head biker bar in the woods.

Yeah … Of course … but I'm not sure if this whole thing's real or not. I don't know if it matters anymore, really.

I don't know … I mean… I'll text you if I feel like they're going to kill me or something.

[gun shots or back firing of a car]

Keep tracking me, I guess … okay … yeah …I love you too.

[hangs up phone]

[turns attention to audience]

Has this ever happened to you?

I'm just kidding. Of course it hasn't.

Hi … I'm Mic Fox.

If you're reading or watching this or whatever, I probably know you personally or something very bad has happened to me. Regardless, thanks for being here to experience whatever the hell *this* is.
– –

To prologue this mess, a little background on me. I grew up in Northwest Ohio — an offensively mild place. If you're not familiar with Ohio, it's Florida with a limiter on it.

And if you don't know what a "limiter" is then damn dawg … you should rent a dirt bike or something. You're telling me you live in *THE* United States and you've never been on a dirt bike? Sure … we may not have healthcare here, but boy … you can just ride a dirt bike around and do wheelies with your friends and if you take the limiter off, that thing's practically a motorcycle, you know.

Ohio's all the freaks of Florida but "oops, all corn!" It's your Juggalo cousin's Bob Segar flavored cover band playing at some bar called *The Regal Beagle* or *Wooly Bully's* for like … 44,000 square miles.

Don't get me wrong, I love it. It's fascinating. I even wrote a book about it. It's called *Midwestern Pulp.* It came out in 2022 and no one read it.

Who woulda thought a book celebrating one of the most unseasoned, undereducated, TV-centric, gray-skied places in these United States wouldn't get read? I mean … there are people who are *in* the book, who KNOW they're *in* the book, who didn't *read* the book. That's how few people read this book.

In the process of writing *Midwestern Pulp,* I'd talked myself into moving back to Ohio from Tennessee. I'd talked myself into believing that there's a bottomless untapped well of potential in Ohio and other places that don't fancy themselves … well … fancy. Upon moving here I was struck with the fact that I *may* be the only one here who believes this to be true. And sure, I've been in a writer's rut since we moved up here. And I suppose I didn't … I don't know … fully consider the financial implications of relocating to a region that's been economically stagnant since the Eisenhower administration. But I'm an optimistic guy. There's opportunity for things here. There's room for goodness! But like I said, I *might* be the only person who believes that. And yeah … sure … I guess there's a … loneliness in that…

[introspective self-doubting pause]

ANYWAY … I say all of *this* because *this book,* unfortunately, is the catalyst for the rest of the bullshit you're about to experience tonight.

About a year ago, I was approached to by an elderly gentleman who claimed to have read my book and wanted me to help him "ghost-write" his memoir. This was instantly alarming to me because ya know ... this book maybe sold 200 copies, and I don't know anyone who knows this guy. But sure ... even now, as I say this, it doesn't sound *that* crazy. People ghost-write for folks all the time. Chat GPT exclusively ghost-writes for every high school student in this country. Ghost-writing a novel for an eccentric old man doesn't sound *that wild*. But that's the issue with Ohio and fly-over-country in general ... we phrase our shit so it doesn't *sound* THAT WILD.

"Oh yeah ... I helped this guy write his book or somethin."

We down play it.

We make it sound believable.

But no ... that's not how it fuckin happened. That's the end result, I guess. But what *really* happened isn't *that* believable. Life isn't THAT believable.

It's FUCKIN WILD.

And until we start sayin the wild shit out loud, we're going to keep believing that this entire part of the world and the lives of the folks that live here really are the boring,
"Oh you know me ... another day, another dollar."
"Nothin ever changes 'round here" type-shit that people say it is.

So I'm here tonight to say the wild shit out loud. And I know this aint no book and I know this aint no memoir but without further ado ... these are

The Possibly Impossible Lives of Charles "Chuy" Chalmers

Safety

Mic   So let me walk it back for you a bit.

It's late summer 2022 and I've just received a ticket for not
having a life jacket aboard my "aquatic vessel" while
boating on a body of water that's regulated by the state. By
"aquatic vessel" I obviously mean inflatable raft that I'd
purchased online while drinking with friends and by "body
of water regulated by the state" I mean the creek that goes
behind my buddy's apartment complex … which yes, I
suppose is more of a river that is, I suppose, a tributary that
eventually dumps into Lake Erie. But still … I didn't want
to pay a ticket that costs more than this stupid raft. So I
asked the polite-yet-firm Ohio-Wildlife-Boat-Officer-Guy
if there was a way out of the ticket other than paying it. And
instead of asking me for a crude sexual favor, he told me
that I could attend a *Boating Safety Course* that Ohio
Wildlife puts on once a month.

So here I sit, in a folding chair in a marine supply store in a
shopping plaza next to an Outback Steakhouse at 7:30pm
on a Friday in late September somewhere west of
Cleveland.

Aside from a group of adults standing in the back and the
man teaching the class who has spliced Ohio Wildlife's
educational video with clips of him and his buddies riding
jetskis around, I am the only adult present. Other than
myself, the class is composed of kids between the ages of
12 and 16 who are all too familiar with the concept of
sitting in a lecture style situation and taking notes while
some weird tan dude talk about his jetski crew.

As I periodically look around the room, I realize the adults
standing in the back are the parents of my underage
classmates and they're here, not because they received
boating violations on their inflatable rafts but because they
need their kids to get boating licenses so they can get
loaded with their buddies on the boat while the kid operates
the vessel. It's a good plan really. I respect it.

There is one adult who I keep catching eyes with. He's an older man – older than the rest of the adults.

You know – when a man sits somewhere between 50 and 85 but you can't quite tell because he's eccentric.

He keeps yucking it up with these parents and whenever the instructor turns to give the man 'KEEP IT DOWN eyes,' the man mouths the word 'SORRY' to the instructor then turns and makes eye contact with me as well. The first time it happens, I think nothing of it. The second time, "whatever, the dude's just a weirdo." But I start refusing his gaze after the 4th time this happens. He's definitely doing it on purpose by this point and I don't want no trouble from some weird old man while I'm trying to cheat off some 6th graders boating exam.

The man disappears by the time I wrap up my test. Not that I'm worried about anything. I have run-ins with strange rangers all the time. But it's 9-o-clock at this point and I'm ready to have a normal rest of the weekend. I thank the instructor, who gives me his card in case I ever "wanted to come cruise with his P-Dub Club."

"P-Dub" being 'P.W.'

'P.W.' Meaning 'Personal Watercraft'

'Personal Watercraft' meaning jetskis.

Being invited via business card to go ride around with some jetski gang is probably one of the wilder interactions I've had but it's nothing compared to everything that follows. Regardless I grab my gear and make my way towards the car.

I drop my keys in the parking lot and as I bend down to grab them, somebody whistles. Like, loud cat-call whistles. I look up, assuming it's a buddy of mine who's always taking any excuse to cat-call a friend out-and-about. I laugh, look up, and instead of seeing an old friend, I see that weird old man from the class and some other more gangly stranger hanging sloppily off of him. I have no desire to interact with them, so I send them a polite farmers wave, letting them know that I wasn't interested.

As I start my car, I'm keeping a lookout for these dudes as all of our interactions have been bizarre and they've become annoying if not slightly predatory. But they break from my sight-line and all the sudden there's a knock on my driver's side window.

If these guys were even slightly more intimidating, I'd be pretty concerned. But there was something about them that was non-threatening enough for me to roll my window down a touch.

Mic   Can I help you?

Chuy   So sorry about the cat-call. My partner here is absolutely classless. Harmless but classless.

Goosh   Chuy, Stop!

Chuy   You stop! First you whistle at him like a little pig then we come knocking on his door in the nighttime in this fucking parking lot like a couple of night-walkers.

Goosh   Night Walkers? Ha! You wish you had the eyes of a 1960s Robert Taylor, you old man!

Chuy   Hit me where it hurts, why don't you![1]

Mic   Guys! What can I do for ya? What is this? I don't think I know either of you and yes, I'm annoyed at this point and I'd like to move on with my weekend.

Chuy   I am so sorry. You're Mike Fox aren't you?

Mic   What?
Why?
Who's asking?

Goosh   Oh my God! He said it like the movies! *Who's askin?*

Chuy   *Midwestern Pulp,* right? That was the funniest thing I've read in ages. My friend got it for me and usually I don't listen to this friend. But he said it was hilarious and I didn't even know that he knew how to read. So I gave it a shot and boom, I read the whole thing in one night. Stayed up til dawn reading it. It was *so good!*

Goosh   Yeah. Then he wouldn't shut the fuck up about it.

---

[1] Chuy and Goosh speak over each other constantly. I hope you can hear this as you read it.

Chuy   *Shut up, Goosh!* Sorry about him. He's a sass and he had one too many *Fostahs at the Outback,* if you know what I mean.[2]

Mic   Hey, thanks for reading it.

Chuy   It's always funny to see an adult in those boating classes cus it means you did something stupid that was probably pretty fun. But the wildlife cops are a buncha queens and they'll give *anybody* a ticket.

Goosh   Who you callin a queen!?

Chuy   *Shut the fuck up, Goosh!* Go wait in the car if you're not going to be nice!

Goosh   Relax, babe. You're always simping for these cisses. They can be funny too, ya know.

Chuy   I don't even know the words you're saying. This new woke-talk is *classless,* Goosh. So sorry to bicker in front of you. I just saw you in the class and thought it was you. Then I saw the bumper sticker on the car and said, "That's gotta be him." And here you are. It's you. You're him.

---

[2] The Australian accent here is just horrible.

Mic   Yep … it's me. Thanks for reading the book. I'm sure I'll put something else out soon enough. Keep an eye on the website and stuff. Nice to meet you guys.[3]

Chuy   Oh yes … we should let you go. Sorry this was the most awkward meeting ever. I PROMISE WE'RE NOT CRAZY OR ANYTHING. Jesus. That's exactly what a crazy person would say. Maybe I had one too many *mahtinis at the Outback*[4] … Anyway … I'm Charlie this is my partner, Goosh.

Mic   Nice to meet you Charlie. I'm Mic … like Mickey Mouse.

Chuy   Mick! Not Mike. Mic. Sorry.

Mic   And did you say his name is "GOOSH?"[5]

Chuy   Yes, Goosh. He's a bitch. But I've never known a funnier bitch. I'm sure we'll see you around, Mic.

Mic   Yes. Nice to meet you, Charlie.

---

[3] I'm obviously being short here. I need them away from me. They're stressing me out and I'm trapped in my car in the parking lot of an Outback Steakhouse and I hate it and hell is real and my wife's going to love this story.

[4] Again … with the Australian accent. Why?

[5] Who the fuck is called, Goosh? Why?

Chuy   Please … call me Chuy. All my friends call me Chuy. And you can call me Chuy cus we're Friends now.

Mic   Ok, Chuy. Yall have a nice night.

I Told You My Wife's Going to Love This Story

[back at the house, Mic and Molly watch TV from a couch and chat while cruising on their phones]

Molly   I don't like that story.

Mic   [laughing] Which part?

Molly   All of it. These guys sound like creeps.

Mic   They were creeps.

Molly   But what, you're not creeped out because they're *just* freaky old predators?

Mic   They seemed harmless enough. They were just … strange. That was the first stranger I've met who's read the book.

Molly   So WHAT? *Now* you're hanging out with old queeny dudes at boating stores just because they liked your book?! Well … I'm glad you've found your people, babe. I'm sure you'll all be *very happy* together.[6]

Mic   You're being such a bully, babe.

---

[6] She lays it on like this through the whole scene.

Molly   If you can't handle *THIS*, there's NO WAY you can handle *getting got* by some OLD DUDES in the parking lot of the *Outback Steakhouse, baaaabe.*

Mic   Easy! Easy! This is good source material at the very least. I can get something out of that freaky little interaction.

Molly   Yeah! I'm sure if you wanted, you could have freaky little interactions every day of the week in the parking lot of the OUTBACK STEAKHOUSE, you bitch.

Mic   Alright, I get it. Are you just going to keep this up until we go to bed?

Molly   *That's what your new friends said to you before they kissed you goodnight, huh?*[7]

Mic   Okay … okay …"

---

[7] I think she's doing Darrell Hammond doing Sean Connery on Celebrity Jeopardy on Saturday Night Live here. But it's hard to tell, honestly.

Mic   [to audience]

At this point I realize I need to change the subject or
Molly's going to dog me for this all night. So I reach for
my phone in an attempt to find some internet trash that
will distract her from the taste of blood she's found in my
little story. I catch a glimpse of my *inbox* which is usually
just emails trying to get me to buy more art supplies or
bootleg Grateful Dead merch, but on top of all the spam,
there's an email submitted via the 'Contact' form of my
website.

Mr. Fox

It was lovely making your acquaintance this evening. Again, my apologies for Goosh. He's harmless, but regardless, I am embarrassed. So sorry.

I'm sure you're a busy man, but I wanted to pick your brain on a project that I've been working on for some time and wondered if we might be able to sit down in the coming weeks for a chat.

I've been lucky enough to live quite a life with the short time I've been given on this earth. I've been slowly collecting stories of all my travels and adventures but haven't quite figured out how to compile them into something worthy of their salt.

That is, until I read your book. I love the irreverence. I love the dialog. I love the sauce. And I think your sauce would take my sandwich of a story to the next level.

This is an unusual ask for me, but I'm getting older and don't have the time to NOT ASK questions when they pop into my head. So if this sounds AT-ALL interesting or like something you'd be into, know that I'm quite serious about putting a book together and I think my story and the compensation I'm prepared to offer you for your assistance are well worth your wile.

Feel free to give me a call.

Chuy Chalmers

216.555.6942

Molly   Oh, this is getting good. What're you going to do?

Mic   Ha! What do *you* think I should do?

Molly   He said he 'wants your sauce,' babe. I say you give him your sauce.[8]

Mic   Jesus Christ…

Molly   Sauce him up, babe.[9]

Mic   Seriously though, should I call him?

Molly   What do you think he wants you to do?

Mic   I don't know. The energy is like he wants me to help him write his memoirs or something. I'm not qualified to do anything like that.

Molly   Well … he sounds like a freaky dude. You're kind of a freaky dude. Maybe he actually read your book and liked it … Or maybe he just WANTS YOUR SAUCE NEAR AND POSSIBLY ON—

Mic   Stop. Stop. You always take it there.

Molly   Like *you* wouldn't?! You're *begging* for it, babe.

---

[8] Here we go again…

[9] "Sauce him up" is kinda funny though.

Mic   What do you think I should do?

Molly   I think we should at least google his
         ass and see if anything weird pops up.

[frantically Googling]

Molly   *This* is the guy?! This weird old man
         with the Coke bottle glasses?

Mic   That's definitely him.

Molly   It looks like he's just on a bunch of
         arts council, philanthropic, yada-yada
         museum-board-of-directors   sorta
         stuff. Does he have like an old-money
         vibe or what?

Mic   I don't know. He was hanging around at
         a prop-shop attached to an Outback out
         in the burbs. I didn't have time to
         catch a vibe.

Molly   Was he *in* that class with you or just
         hanging out?

Mic   I think he was just hangin out.

Molly   WHY?

Mic   I don't know, honestly. Like … he
         seemed to know a lot about the class.
         Like … he hangs out there a lot? Maybe?
         He made a weird comment about how *'it's
         always funny seeing adults in that
         class'* or something.

Molly   Oh … so he's a weirdo-arts-philanthropist who hangs out in the burbs trolling for young thangs in the parking lot of the Outback. Seems chill. What did you say his partner's name was?

Mic   Goosh. I was certain I was hearing that wrong, but it's right here in this email.[10]

Molly   GOOSH?! Man's name is *Goosh?* That's fucked up, babe.

Mic   I know. Should I holler back at him?

Molly   I mean … what's the risk in a phone call? It's like you said, at the very least this is good source material. And hey … I think you DESERVE a freaky phone call with some weird old man. This is why we moved back here, right? So you could mingle with some absolute freaks in their natural habitat, right?

Mic   Dammit.

[to black]

--SOME TIME LATER

Molly   Babe! Babe!

---

[10] Again, Who the fuck is called, "Goosh?" It's no good.

Mic   [waking up frantically] What!? What happen? You okay?

Molly   Yeah. I think this guy's a freak but you should call him tomorrow.

Mic   What time is it?

Molly   Game time, bitch. I don't know … 3:30 or something.

Mic   *Fuck.* You been up this whole time? Go to bed.

Molly   Dude … look at all these photos.

[Molly flips her phone around to reveal a Pinterest collage she's made of Chuy Chalmers.]

Mic   What the fuck is wrong with you?

Molly   Dude … look at his hands in all these pics.

Mic   [to the audience]

        Of the 20-some photos, Chuy's old ass is either subtly flipping the bird or flashing a "shocker" (in the style of an ornery teenage boy) in almost every single picture.

        [back to Molly]

        So you think, because of this man's willingness to hide blatant profanity in plain sight, I'd be a good match in helping him put his memoir together? If that's even what he wants.

Molly   Sort of. If these pics are any indication of what kinda creature this guy is … I don't know … he's like a character from your book. Certifiable. I mean … look at this one!

Mic   [to the audience]

She shows me a picture of Chuy standing with John Glenn and Neil Armstrong, all three of them laughing with their arms around each other, Chuy with two middle fingers up like Nixon flashing peace-signs after resigning the presidency.[11]

[back to Molly]

That's fucking wild. I'll holler at him tomorrow, I guess. Please don't wake me up to show me photos of old men in the middle of the night anymore.

Molly   Oh … I thought that's what you liked, *daddy*.

Mic   Don't wake daddy, *mommy*.

Molly   Ew … '*mommy*' is bad.

Mic   Yeah she is.

Molly   Stop.

[to black]

---

[11] This is the kinda shit that gets me into trouble. I love stuff like this. The profanity. The juxtaposition. I couldn't have written it better.

--SOME MORE TIME LATER

[The next morning, Molly's shuffling around loudly while carrying a laptop. Mic sits.]

Mic   … but It's not even 9-o-clock.

Molly   Old people are up way earlier than that. Don't be a little bitch. Put that shit on speaker. I wanna hear what this weirdo sounds like.

[Mic dials phone 216-555-6942. Rings twice then a woman with a gum-smackin mid-20th century midwestern-secretary voice answers.[12]]

Sandy   Good morning! Dr. Chalmers' Office. Sandy speaking.[13]

Mic   Hi Sandy! My name's Mic Fox. I got an email from Mister … or I guess … Doctor Chalmers and was just fol—

Sandy   Mr. Fox! Chuy's been expecting your call. He's out and about right now but told me to set up a time for you to come meet up at the house.

Mic   Oh … I was just looking to hear a little bit more about what he was thinking … regarding what he … I don't want to waste anyone's time.

---

[12] If that makes sense.

[13] Yall are gonna like Sandy.

Sandy   I *totally* understand. Chuy doesn't really talk business over the phone or work well on the computer. To tell you the truth … *I* actually transcribed that email for him the other night. We've got a great set-up over here. The breeze off the lake is awesome this time of year and the earliest trees are just starting to turn. Chuy told me that he's happy to send a car for you and I've got a check sitting in front of me that I'm supposed to overnight to you if you're able to come up for a meeting at the home office.

Mic   Oh … you don't need to do that.

Sandy   *Sure we do.* Time is money, Mr. Fox. It's all we have. You can't just give away your most valuable asset expecting nothing in return. I'm sure you're plenty busy but I promise that it'll be worth your time. How's this … let's plan on lunch this upcoming Wednesday. I'll overnight you the check this evening and if that number is intriguing enough, shoot me an email and I'll send you the address for Wednesday.

Mic   Wednesday would work for me but seriously … you don't need to send a check or a car or anything like that.

Sandy   I look forward to meeting you Mr. Fox. We'll be in touch before Wednesday.

Wednesday

Mic   [to the audience]

I'd love to disclose details of the money they overnighted but it seems classless and you beautiful people are too classy for such numerical drivel. Beyond that, you're still here. Which means I'm still writing it. Which means the number on that check was large enough to get us this far. Not large enough to make me a better writer. But ... alas.

I refused the car service they offered. It was a kind and professional gesture. But in my limited experience, when dealing with wealthy weirdos, it's in your best interest to have personal means of transport for a speedy get-away if you should find yourself in a Jordan Peele *'Get Out'* style scenario

As I turn onto Chuy's street, my GPS hits me with

```
"Your destination is on the right."
```

I take a moment to slow down and admire the view.

Every house on Chuy's block has an unobstructed view of Lake Erie. The houses don't back up to the lake, but sit atop of a cliff directly *across the street* from the lake ... like if a *Bond* villain had next door neighbors and drove a 12-year-old Bimmer rather than a submarine or something.

The houses on the street are a mix of tastefully redone mansions from the early 1900s and new-money nightmares decorated in the style of "I wish we had a castle but I covered the house with \$400,000 of river stone veneer instead."

Chuy's house sits somewhere in between.

It's a beautiful old colonial monster with a giant three-story concrete "modern" porch dropped on the front of it. The house looks like Maine and the porch looks like Florida.[14]

The porch is a hot mess on it's own right, but you hardly notice it because the *amount of yard art* distracts from the architectural atrocity.

And I'm not talking about a freaky little gnome or some swinger-signaling flamingos here and there.[15] I'm talking about a beyond-eccentric flex of wealth in a style I'd call

CONCRETE SCULPTURAL MAXIMALISM

Off the top of my head, I remember... A family of concrete bigfoots, a concrete frog the size of a cow, and a small army of small concrete sheep all wearing different uniforms.[16] [17]

---

[14] If that makes sense.

[15] There are also plenty of those, mind you.

[16] Like if the *Village People* were concrete sheep and there were twenty of them.

[17] You know when you're driving through some small town on the way to some weird cabin that your grandparents booked for the "family getaway" that you're forced to attend and you pass by a strange little house that's also a business that sells concrete geese and fountains for ponds and tombstones? Then everything they've got for sale is set up in rows on the lawn right there on the road? This is like if that spot had 270° lake views and a cocaine problem.

I park on the street between the lake and the house and begin to navigate my way through the concrete animal jungle in front of the giant triple decker porch. I ping my location and send it to Molly. (Partially for security reasons but really in hopes that she can see a *Google Street View* of this mess.)

Sandy   *[from a nondescript balcony]*

        Mickey! Mickey!

[Mic tries to place where the voice is coming from]

Sandy   Oh, sorry sweetie! Up here!

        THEY'RE OUT OF THE BOAT, SUG! I'LL COME DOWN AND WALK YOU OUT THERE!

Mic   [to himself]

        Jesus. I'm gonna get trapped out on a boat with these freaks.

Sandy   [now on the ground level, (within 3 seconds mind you) she sneaks up behind Mic and scares the shit outta him]

        Howdy, partner! Oh my GOODNESS, I am so sorry I scared you.[18]

---

[18] She scared the piss outta me. I still have no idea how she got down from that balcony so fast. I know she explains it here in a sec, but it still doesn't fully make sense to me. Though ... this whole story is kinda like that so ... whatever..

Mic   [laughing nervously and gesturing towards the balcony]

       Oh, it's fine. I'm good. How did you— You were just—

Sandy Oh! There's a big slide that goes from the porch down to the steps of the dock. It's the quickest way down here. I was bitching to Chuy as they were building this porch about how there's no quick way to get down to the yard and if the puppers has to tinkle or drop a deuce, I can't just tell her to hold it then go back into the house and down all those steps and then out through the patio and then across the street to the little grassy patch by the dock steps. She don't even speak English. She's part German Shepherd. Oh my lord, I forgot to officially introduce myself. I'm Sandy. We spoke on the phone and this is Lil Ms. Dog.[19]

       So instead of putting in steps from the porch like a normal person, Chuy had the contractor build a big ol' playground slide that wraps around the back of the house and drops Lil Ms. Dog down by the little patch of grass by the dock.

[19] Sandy is a woman between the ages of 45 and 70 with the largest perm I've ever seen in person. It could be a wig, but if so, it may be the most expensive wig I've ever seen. At the time of this conversation, she's holding what, at first glance, appears to be a massive Corgi, but upon closer inspection it appears to be a full sized German Shepherd with comically short legs aka Lil Ms. Dog.

Mic   And that's how you got down here so
          fast?

Sandy   Bingo. Lil Ms. Dog loves it and I think
          it keeps me young. Never get old
          Mickey. It's some bullshit. Ain't that
          right Ms. Thang?[20]

          Anyway … I'll show you down to the
          boat.

Mic   [to audience]

          We walk back down the same steps I'd just walked up,
          past my car and across the street to some overgrown
          brush that's been growing on this cliff. I follow Sandy
          through a small gap in the brush that I wouldn't have
          noticed otherwise. We walk through a long, beyond
          overgrown trellis with vibes that can only be described
          as   "Savannah-Georgia-Cemetery-Wedding-Murder-
          Location."

          The level in which this trellis/hallway thing is overgrown
          has me temporarily forgetting that it is, in fact, the
          middle of the day.

          It has my senses dialed to 'haunted corn maze.' I fully
          expect Chuy or this Goosh person to emerge from the
          brush with a chainsaw or perhaps a comically large
          martini glass any moment.

          We reach the end of this trellis and begin our decent
          down a series of very slippery, very old wooden steps.

---

[20] She says this directly into to the dog's nose provoking sloppy, wet, face licks and
a foul smell as this poor dog is old as hell.

The amount of steps gives me time to realize how far above the lake this cliff really is. As I hang on to the moss-covered handrail, stepping cautiously onto every slimy sludgy stair, Sandy and Lil Ms. Dog seem to be floating effortlessly–as if they're skiing down some strange snow-covered mountain.[21]

After what feels like every bit of five minutes, the steps spit us out at a small private beach and a long dock that extends out into Mother Erie. At the end of the dock sits, what appears to be, an old red tug boat. I don't know a whole lot about boats (despite my previously mentioned inflatable raft) but as I mindlessly follow Sandy and Lil Ms. Dog down the dock, I realize I've never seen a boat quite like this. It looks more like a cartoon than anything.

```
Chuy    She's great, isn't she?

Mic     Yeah! She's … great.[22]

Goosh   She's      not      thaaat      great.
```

---

[21] Or how you know in the Disney film, *Tarzan*, the one with the Phil Collins soundtrack, when Tarzan is kinda surfing on those branches through the jungle. So sick. I think Rosie O'Donnell did the voice of someone in that movie. Remember when Rosie had that daytime talk show in the 90s. My mom loved that show.

[22] I'm not sure if he's talking about the boat or Sandy at this point so I weigh my options. "She's great," works.

Mic   [to audience]

          All of my interactions with these people thus far have
          been similarly and upsettingly theatrical. It's like
          they're reciting lines from a play. Not in a way where
          it's been rehearsed but in a way where they present like
          characters on a reality television program. They play to
          the camera. They cheat to the audience. It's upsetting.
          But we're already here. And I guess this is *kind of* a
          play. So let's lean into it, shall we?

Sandy   At ease, boys. Don't try so hard.
          You'll scare the kid.

          [winks at Mic then loudly whispers…]

          Seriously, these queens are harmless.
          They're just showing off.

Mic   Wow … I mean … it really is somethin.

Chuy   It's all Goosh. He's been restoring
          this thing for years. You wouldn't
          believe what it looked like when we
          got ahold of it. I had no idea it'd
          become something like this. But Goosh
          is like that. He gets his mind set on
          something and polishes that idea til
          it's … I don't know … a beautiful old
          tugboat, I spoze.

Goosh   Wow Chuy … you have *such* a way with
          words.

Chuy   Oh stop, babe! I was paying you a
          compliment.

          Well Mr. Fcx, let's have a tour shall
          we!

Mic   [to audience]

           Goosh then leads the three of us and Lil Ms. Dog around
           the boat–speaking about all the restoration and detail
           work he's put into it over the past 20 years. He tells me
           about how Sandy made him and Chuy sleep on the boat
           after she caught the two of them fooling around together.
           Sandy chimes in periodically to add details…

Sandy   I knew Chuy was bent when I married
           him. We were open that way. But I
           wanted to see how committed Goosh was
           to this relationship. It's one thing
           to be knockin knees. It's another to
           handle the choppy seas. Oh my god that
           rhymes. I should be a writer like you,
           Mickey.

Mic   [to audience. Sandy, Chuy, and Goosh continue in the
             background]

           We now find ourselves on the upper deck of this
           beautiful 100-year-old tugboat sitting at a table that
           matches every other piece of wood on the boat. If you
           told me it came this way, I'd believe you. If you told me
           that Goosh carved it with his teeth then sealed it with a
           homemade stain derived from the algae blooms and salt
           mines of Lake Erie, I'd believe that too. Why not? It's
           strange enough that I'm here on this boat with these
           characters, I might as well just take what they're saying
           as gospel and keep it pushing. Regardless …

Sandy   Are you writing this down, Mickey.
           This is important.

Mic   Oh sorry … wait, what am I supposed to
           be writing?

[The three of them chuckle in unison. Lil Ms.
 Dog lets out a single bark then starts
 licking Chuy on the mouth.]

Goosh   Miss Dog! Stop it. Dog's mouths are
         supposed to be clean. Quit kissin that
         dirty old man.

Sandy   [to Mic]

         I'm kidding sweetie. You zoned out
         there. Chuy's been zoning out a bit
         himself these days.

         We haven't even touched on why you're
         here! Let's get to it. *Cheers!*

[They all hold up giant glasses of sparkling
 tangerine colored wine on ice.]

Chuy   Yes, let's get to it. Shall we? I don't
         want to take up too much of your time.
         I want you to help me write my stories,
         Mr. Fox. I thought *Midwestern Pulp* was
         so cute and talky. And I figure, I'm
         cute and talky and you'd be great at
         helping me get some of these stories
         on paper.

Goosh   *That,* and he's illiterate, Mic. The
         poor bastard can't read or write for
         shit.

Sandy   Be nice!

Goosh   I'm serious, Mic. Chuy's made his
         entire fortune talkin and walkin
         around like he's some intellectual,
         but he can't read a lick.

Mic   Well, how'd he read my book then?

Goosh How do you think?

Sandy He made us read it to him.

Mic   What? It's not worth *all that*. It's not *that good* a book!

Goosh We fucking know, Mic! We're the ones who read it to him. [refilling his wine]

Mic   Well Jesus, I'm sorry to hear that. Can you really not read, Chuy?

Chuy   I'm afraid not. See, I was born into a *very poor household* and had to fend for myself at a *very young age*. So I never made it to school. I was the youngest of 16 … no … 17 brothers and sisters and of course I picked up some things here and there, but I never quite got the hang of it. Sandy thinks I'm dyslexic. Goosh thinks I'm—

Goosh A nasty dirty old man.

Chuy   Exactly. *See* … I can't take him anywhere. *See, Sandy*. I told you. He's like this all the time now. I should've never brought you into the main house, *you soggy dog!*

[Goosh takes a shrimp, grabs it by the tale between his teeth then bends down to feed the shrimp to Chuy via mouth. He then grabs another shrimp and gestures towards Mic. Mic politely puts his hand up, shake his head, and mouth the words, "I'm good." Goosh blows a kiss at Mic and pops the shrimp into his own mouth.]

Chuy   I'm truly a *self-made man.* I've got stories that need told. If I can do the things I've done, then anyone can. I want to inspire the youth.

Goosh   Inspire them to what … be a slutty, illiterate philanthropist?

Chuy   *Jesus Goosh*, that hurt.

Mic   That's sounds great and all but people, especially young folks don't really *read* anymore. I mean, I like books but maybe a podca…

Goosh   Oh my god, Mic. This old man tried to start a podcast during Covid. *What a nightmare.*[23]

Sandy   *Oh shoot.* I forgot about that. It was horrible, Mic. He had his friend, Eddie, record some music for it and everything. It was so so bad.

---

[23] This round of dialogue about Chuy's podcast cooks at about 200mph. And Chuy just sits there and takes it.

Goosh   [wipes tears from his eyes, laughing.] Mic … *you* would've *loved* it. It was *so bad*. Like … how did *this man* get *this far* in life?

[Podcast starts then gets louder and louder as they talk over it]

Sandy   I'll find you the recordings of the show. You'll need to hear *some* of it if you're going to help him write this book.

Mic   Why was it so bad? Yall seem to talk fine. That's all a podcast is. And it's *way easier* than writing a book.

Goosh   CHEWING WITH CHUY! It was called, *'Chewing with Chuy,'* Mic. And it was just him rambling on and on…

Sandy   Yes. You know when you're at a family reunion and there's an old man there who's maybe your great uncle or somethin and he corners you and talks *AT* you for what feels like hours and you can't get away because no one will come save you and before you know it, you've backed up enough where he has you physically trapped?

Goosh   Yes. And he's just *talking and spitting and rambling and drooling and chewing AND CHEWING AND CHEWING AND SPITTING AND TALKING AND CHEWING!*

Sandy   Yes. THE *CHEWING AND TALKING AND SPITTING AND CHEWING…*

Goosh   Yes. It was like that but a podcast. And he thought people would *want* to listen to it.

Sandy   [wiping tears and trying to catch her breath] Yes … and his friend's music in the back was so crazy. And it wasn't like instrumental music, Mic. He was just talking over this man *singing.* And he's not a great singer, Mic. He's like a bad karaoke DJ type. And the music's playing at full volume and Chuy's just *rambling* over it."

Goosh   It really felt like something you'd see in a David Lynch movie. It was a full-blown car wreck. It was so scary and over-stimulating and underwhelming. It should be studied. *You're sick, Chuy.*

[Podcast stops]

Sandy   It was a true mess. You woulda loved it, Mic.

Chuy   Yeah … so we tried the podcast. But I don't think it's the right format for me. That market's too saturated anyway.

[Sandy and Goosh both laugh.]

Goosh   Yeah … 'too saturated' … *That* was the problem.

Chuy   So, I'm thinking book, Mic. It's a
         memoir. Memoir's are good. What do you
         think? You wanna help an old man turn
         his stories into a book?

Mic   I mean, how big of a book are we
         talking? How serious are you about
         this? Am I ghost writing? Are we…

Sandy   Chuy's prepared to offer you a
         substantial guarantee upfront, then
         50% of any advance we may procure on a
         book deal and 40% of all royalties.[24]

Mic   Woah. That's pretty generous … You're
         serious about this, huh?

         [to audience]

         Sandy writes down a number on a napkin (the guarentee)
         and passes it to me. I look at it then back at her. Then at
         Chuy. Then at Goosh (who is now finishing his second
         giant glass of ice wine). Then back at Sandy.

Sandy   So beyond *that* guarantee, we've got a
         number of friends in the publishing
         houses out east that are interested
         conceptually but Chuy was *ADAMANT* that
         you were on board. They offered him
         some seasoned ghost-writers but, like
         we said earlier, he doesn't *read* a
         whole lot…

---

[24] I know we're getting in the weeds here. But numbers like this are kind of
unprecedented. Especially for an unknown author. THIS is how I get into a mess like
this. THIS is why the world is the way it is. People do *DUMB* stuff for money. Myself
included, I guess.

Chuy   Because I don't know how to read.[25]

Sandy   Right. We'd want to get started fairly soon. I'm sure you're very busy [26], but if you can make the time, he'd love to hit the ground running in hopes that you can have a draft done by the Spring.

Chuy   I know that sounds fast, Mic. But I don't want a traditional memoir. I just want some stories. I want *YOU* to tell the stories of *ME* telling *YOU* the stories before I forget them...

[awkward pause. Chuy starts laughing. No one else does.]

---

[25] Looking back, the nonchalantness here should've been a red-flag. The foreshadowing is hangover inducing, to say the least.

[26] I'm not.

> Listen, here's how I see it … We spend about two or three weeks chatting it up during the day. You can record these conversations or whatever. Then me and Goosh, Sandy and Little Ms. Dog go to Savannah for the winter. We'll be around to talk on the phone if you want but I'd rather you take all the creative liberties you need to put a good book together. We'll meet back up in the spring when we get back to town and I'll have Goosh and Sandy here read me your draft. What you think?[27]

Mic   I mean … I think that *sounds* do-able.[28]

Chuy   Oh … Mr. Fox … I have no doubts about it! I've lived my whole life going on gut feeling, alone. This is going to be just lovely! I'd be tickled to have you apart of this. Whatdayasay? [Chuy extends his hand]

Mic   [to audience]

> My natural inclination when someone extends their hand is to shake it. I don't make a lot of 'deals.' Almost every handshake I've ever made might-as-well-have-been a high-five. I'm typically a fairly unserious, contract-less hand-shaker. But alas…

> [to Chuy, shaking his hand]

---

[27] Again. This is too enticing. It's too "low-stakes." It's *actually* too good to be true. And that's no good. People always say that like it's a good thing. *"It's too good to be true!"* Yeah … muhfucka … it probably is!

[28] Yeah … *TOO DO-ABLE, you idiot.*

```
Hey  …  if  it's  as  simple  and
straightforward as talking and writing
down some of your stories, I'd be happy
to help in any way I can.
```

[to audience, still holding Chuy's hand]

Looking back, this is where my Midwestern-niceties really start biting me in the ass. But hey … we got a story out of it, right?

[Silence. Stage fades black.]

Right, guys?

Right, Guys?

Mic   [to audience]

Up to this point, I've been trying to articulate and justify how I got myself into this position in the first place. I'm doing it for myself as much as I am for yall. There needs to be some sort of catalyst to how or why I find myself in the position of hanging with these weirdos for the times that follow. But I feel like it's taking too long.

So I'll spare you too much more explanation and verbalized self-doubt by just making up a lie to push this story along:

I had my wife, Molly, who *now happens to be a lawyer* (for the sake of the story), review the contract Sandy sends over that afternoon. She finds my re-hashing of Chuy's proposition amusing, intriguing, and concerning.

These fools are flashing a decent amount of money at me (certainly more than I'd ever planned on making off of my writing). And that's exciting but I also know that there are definitely better and more professional ways to go about getting a memoir written … ESPECIALLY if they already have connections in the publishing world.

Molly says the contract is pretty straight-forward if not blatantly in my favor. The guarantee is solid enough for me to take a crack at it and hell … if I can just tape-record Chuy monologuing and dictate it back, the book'll hit 200 pages in a matter of a couple hours. I figure he's got more than enough stories to tell and it's not like he wants me to live in his basement and follow him around or anything. I'm just writing down a few stories. Right?[29]

---

[29] I'm obviously *really* talking myself into it here.

So Molly tweaks a couple phrasing issues in the contract and we send it back to them. Within the hour, Sandy accepts our edits on Chuy's behalf and resends the contract for us to sign.

Molly holds her breath as I sign it then starts laughing.

Molly   Dude … I hope this goes well and we don't end up dead in the lake or something.

Mic   Babe … Why would you say that?

Molly   I don't know. Rich people are scary, dawg. This dude doesn't even know how to *read?!* Why do we trust this contract? Aren't there all sortsa 'isms about a contract only being as good as the people making the deals or something?

Mic   Jesus, babe. I *just* signed the contract. You said it was good and you're *definitely a lawyer* in this scenario. Why are you bringing all of this up *after* I *just* signed it? You don't think I've thought about these people being too crazy to work with? You don't think … that I think … that this sounds too good to be true?!

Molly   I know … I know. But you *NEED* this.

Mic   What do you mean?

Molly   You know … you've been between projects since we moved up here. You've been waiting for something like this.

Listen … I thought you were crazy moving us to Ohio. But once we settled in, I thought, "You know … he's right. These ARE *real people*." Sure … they're freaks. But they're *REAL* freaks. No one's "putting on." No one's "playing cowboy." It's just midwestern salty freaks as far as the eye can see. That's kind of your life source, babe. These are your people. And yall are *just* bored enough to invent strange and fucked up ways to make your lives exciting.

This is exactly what you say you want to write about. You can't bitch out now, just because "rich people are scary" or "things seem too good to be true."

So what if they are. Write about it. It's funny. It's real. Even if it's not.

[Landline Phone starts ringing.]

Mic   The phone's ringing.

Molly   Why is the phone ringing?

Mic   I didn't even know we had a landline.

Molly   You'd better answer it.

Mic   I'm not answering that phone. Fuck no.

Molly   This is your fucking play/book-thing buddy, you'd better answer that haunted-ass phone.

[Mic answers phone. Stage immediately flips into a psychedelic, time-warpy, liquid-mess… transporting Mic to Chuy's house.]

He's Gone

[on Chuy's boat]

Sandy   Oh Mic … Thank God![30]

Mic   What's going on? I got here as soon
        as I could.

Sandy   He's gone, Mic! He's gone!

Mic   Who's gone?

Sandy   Chuy! He's gone, Mic![31]

Mic   Oh, Sandy … I'm so sorry.

Sandy   You've gotta find him, Mic! You've
        gotta find him.

Mic   What?... What are you saying.

Sandy   He's gone, Mic! You've GOTTA FIND
        HIM!

Goosh   [Entering scene nonchalantly, he
          reads a piece of paper]

        He's missing, Mic. He's not *dead*.

---

[30] This sequence is so dramatic. Sandy's floating in and out of hysteria while weeping
and talking as fast as she can. Goosh, is seemingly unphased.

[31] You can hear the weeping, right? You can see the mascara, right? Lotta hugging.
Lotta touching. Too much really.

Mic   Oh … What?

Sandy   Is he dead, Goosh?![32]

Goosh   I wish. This little sociopath wants
        us to go on a little scavenger hunt.

Mic   WHAT HAPPENED?!

[Goosh, Sandy and Mic gather around the
   piece of paper, a letter]

--

[The voice of Chuy comes in from off-stage…]

---

[32] The hysterics. Bad drama-club hysterics.

My Dearest Sandy, My Gooshiest Goosh, and Mr. Fox

I hope this letter finds you well, though I'm sure it has not—as I have disappeared myself.

I'm not dead or anything. But I had a full-blown panic attack after our meeting with our new friend, Mic. Please don't blame the boy. He has little to do with this other than helping bring up some truths (or lies, I suppose) about myself, that I've never fully dealt with.

Don't hate me for being a liar, the good times and the love we have shared for all these years has been the most sincere and honest part of my life. But much of my past has been quite the fabrication.

I honestly don't know where to start.

I'm a pathological liar.

So even in this confession, my instinct is to "make something up."

I obviously CAN read and write; as I'm writing this letter to you, right now. And I'm not a self-made man. I'm a spoiled trust-funded old man who was once a young boy whose father made something of HIMSELF. Since his passing, and even before, I've reaped the benefits of HIS life's work, of HIS wealth. And while the philanthropy and the arts endowments have been real, they're just auto-withdrawn from a trust. They'd exist with or without me.

Everything you've ever known about me has been invented from thin-air. I suppose, in THAT way, I AM a self-made man.

Regardless, I need to do some deep soul-searching before I can tell my story. But there are some people who have some real stories about me from the before times. I think a chat with them would be a good place to start.

I can picture Goosh rolling his eyes and Sandy wiping her mascara but please focus, there's not much time! I'm just kidding. I'm fine. But if you do find me ...

Goosh, you get the boat.

Sandy, you get the house.

And Mic, you get a hell of a story if you can pull it off. The guarantee is yours regardless of whether you write a book or not. But if you publish these stories, I'd bet there's some gold in them there hills.

Yours in Peace, Love, Sex, and Violence
Alexa, play Paul Simon, "Sound of Silence"

Chuy

--

Goosh   Dammit, I hate his little poems.

Sandy   Yeah … and it's Simon *AND* Garfunkel.

Mic   What is going on?!

Sandy   "Sound of Silence" is Simon *and*
        Garfunkel not just Paul Simon.

Mic   Who cares! What are yall going to do?

Goosh   [Flipping through a shelf of albums]
        He wants us to visit some old friend
        of his.

Mic   What?

Goosh   He wants us to go visit some old
        friend of his who's gonna tell us
        some story. It's around here
        somewhere…

Sandy   What are you looking for?

Goosh   Got it!

 [Goosh pulls out the Simon and Garfunkel
  album, 'Wednesday Morning, 3 A.M.']

Goosh   See, Mic … we're dealing with a real
        monster here. He wants us to go on
        some wild goose-chase to find his old
        ass.

Sandy   Ah! I see where you're going.

Goosh   You read that letter, Mic, and you
        go, *"Oh man … ya hate to see it. Wish
        I could help you guys. But I don't
        even know this guy or any of his old
        friends. So … best of luck with your
        weird eccentric, lying, sociopath of
        a husband."*

Sandy   Be easy! It's not his fault, Goosh. I
        bet Chuy planned this out before he
        even read Mic's book.

Goosh   I know. You're right. See, Mic. This
        fool loooves treasure hunts. He
        looooves stories. He loves pirates
        and bikers and astronauts and actors
        and trail-trash and writers. He loves
        stories. He runs on it. He always
        said, "If you make life exciting…"

Sandy   "Then it's not fucking boring."

Goosh   Exactly. So I guess his way of doing
        that is to just … I don't know … make
        up his whole past to keep it from
        sounding so fucking lame.

Sandy   To make it more EXCITING, Goosh!

Mic   What is going on!?

Goosh   Catch up or go home, Mic! Chuy's on
        the move! And he's a sick old man
        with a broken brain.

Mic   He's sick?

Sandy   Does "disappearing yourself" sound
        like healthy behavior, Mickey?

Mic   No, I mean, is he "sick sick?" Like
           what's he running from.

Sandy   The same thing you are, Mickey! He's
           running from himself.

Goosh   Exactly. This old man loves clues and
           mysteries and shit like that. And if
           he's on the run, we don't have time
           for any hesitancy.

           Sandy … what'd you say just a second
           ago about Simon and Garfunkel?

Sandy   That the song, "Sound of Silence"
           isn't *JUST* Paul Simon like he says in
           his letter. It's Simon *AND* Garfunkel.

Goosh   Exactly. [going into a bad detective
           voice] And THAT'S where we find our
           first CLUE.

Sandy   I thought "Sound of Silence" was on
           that other album.

Goosh   AH YES! The red harring! Your average
           consumer of mid 60s folk-pop hits
           would say the same, but an avid
           admirer of Paul Simon would KNOW that
           "SOUND of Silence" was NOT *first
           released* or the similarly name
           'SOUNDS of Silence' but on Simon and
           Garfunkel's debut album, 'Wednesday
           Morning, 3 A.M.'

Mic   Oh, maybe there's a note inside!

Goosh   Now, you've got it Mickey! And yes …
         but this rich bitch wouldn't just
         HIDE a clue on the inside of the
         first pressing of their first album,
         an album that was given to him BY
         Paul and Art themselves on his 65th
         birthday. NO, this fool would rather
         write an address in marker on the
         back, destroying a one-of-a-kind
         piece of American music history.

[Goosh reveals the vandalized album art.]
Johnny Ricotta
16808 1/2 Lorain Ave

Mic   Oh, I know where that is.

Sandy   HE'S IN!

Goosh   *I knew he would be!*

Mic   What? No. I'm not going treasure
         hunting for this old man with yall.

Goosh   SURE YOU ARE, MY BOY! A real
         storyteller couldn't pass up a time
         such as this.

[Goosh and Sandy launch into a half-assed
musical number explaining the concept of
the West Park neighborhood in Cleveland]

"West Park is a part of Cleveland where a
bunch of police and firefighters liiiive.

They've got Guinness in the pipes and all
the people are so nice…" [33]

Mic   STOP STOP! We're not doing the
          musical thing. We talked about it.
          Okay. No. No. Stop. Fuck off. No. Get
          outta here.

---

[33] This is a nightmare. I'm so sorry. I told them NO MUSICAL stuff. This is a serious
play. NO MUSICAL STUFF.

Johnny

[to audience]

Sorry. Anyway ... yes ... I guess now we're in West Park. A dominantly Irish neighborhood in beautiful, majestic Cleveland, OH. It's cops, it's firefighters, it's old people, it's Guinness. It's great. But we're not going down to West Park for a pint, today. No. We're going to an Italian restaurant that I've walked by hundreds of times. Honestly, I didn't think it was a functioning business. The windows are completely hazed over and I've never seen anyone come in or out of there. The sign, which has seen better days honestly, just reads,

"ITALIAN"

Cleveland has a large Italian population. It's got neighborhoods that are known internationally for their Italian food. West Park isn't one of those neighborhoods. But here we are ... looking for someone or something called "Johnny Ricotta" in the hopes that they can give us a clue as to the whereabouts of this wild old man. Why am I here? Geez ... I don't know. Why are you here? Why are you still watching this?

[Goosh, Sandy, and Mic enter the restaurant and some bells sound from the door.][34]

Johnny   [from off stage/behind a counter]
       Sorry, we're not open.

Goosh   Sorry to bother you ... we're looking
       for Johnny...

---

[34] This place is dark. And it's covered in dust. Like, an Indiana Jones amount of dust. Not full-blown catacomb dust. But this is definitely not a functioning restaurant.

Johnny   [Entering from off stage wearing an
         apron and carrying a large box. He
         moves through the shadows. We can't
         quite see his face.]

         Sorry to hear that. What can I help
         you with?

Sandy   We're looking for someone called
         "Johnny Ricotta."

Johnny   [pausing] Sorry. Never heard of him.

Mic   [to Goosh] Tell him about the note.

Goosh   I'm not telling him.

Mic   Fuckin tell him.

Goosh   I'm not tellin anyone shit. We don't
         need to jump some old line cook into
         this nonsense.

Sandy   [to Johnny and back into the
         hysterics]

         My husband's missing and he left us
         this address and the name "Johnny
         Ricotta." So I'm hoping someone who
         works here can tell us *what* that
         means or *who* that is or SOMETHING!

[Johnny sets down box and deadbolts the
 door.]

Mic   Fuck this. I'm outta here.

Goosh   Chill, babe.

Johnny   Who are you people?

Sandy   I'm Sandy, this is Goosh, and this is
        Mic Fox.

Mic   Don't give him my last name, Jesus.

Goosh   *Who the fuck are you?*

Johnny That depends. Who's your husband?

Sandy   Chuy Chalmers.

[silence]

[Johnny laughs terrifyingly then everyone
 else starts laughing]

Johnny Well … I haven't heard THAT name in a
        long time. [Johnny, still hanging in
        the shadows, lights up a cigarette.]

Sandy   Do you know where he is?

Johnny Of course not. I don't know *nothin
        about nothin.* That's actually how Mr.
        Chalmers and I know each other.

Goosh   Go on … we don't have all day.

Johnny Well I hope you do. Cus if Mr.
        Chalmers is missing, you're going to
        need more than a day.

Sandy   What's that supposed to mean?

Johnny [stepping into the light. He looks
         like Chuy but wearing an apron.]

        Well, I'll tell you…

[Music starts and Johnny gets up and begins to sing][35]

Mic   Stop! Stop! No. We're not doing the musical thing. I already told them. I know we just met, but we're not doing the musical thing. No one wants that. Stop.

Johnny My apologies.

Mic   It's fine. Just tell us what you're going to tell us. We're already here. Just go ahead.

Johnny Okay … My name is Jesús Cháves. My friends also call me Chuy.

Mic   I hate this.

Sandy   Your name's Chuy too?

Johnny Sí. But no one's called me that since the mid-70s. I was a young man then. Not yet 17.[36]

        My parents moved to the states from Cuba in the late 50s and had me about 10 years later. There weren't a lot of Cubanos here at the time but my father was a fantastic chef and moved here for work under Chef Hector Boiardi.

Mic   Chef Boyardee?

---

[35] Again, so sorry about the musical stuff. It won't happen again.

[36] Here we go…

Johnny   Sí. My father got me into the
         kitchens early. When I was in high
         school, he did a … "job" … for a
         colleague of Mr. Chalmers. But … he
         didn't return from the job.

         Mr. Chalmers felt terribly about this
         and said my mother and I needed to be
         hidden. He said we should leave our
         Cuban roots in the past, as it'd put
         us in grave danger. So we pretend to
         be Italian. I wanted to get a job on
         the east side of town as the Little
         Italy is so lively. But he said the
         real Italians would find us out. So
         he arranged for us to be vaguely
         Italian in the Irish part of town.
         And we've been here since.

Mic   That's wild.

Johnny   Yes. Wild. Mr. Chalmers sent us cash
         in an envelope every other Friday
         since 1976. Always addressed to
         Johnny Ricotta, a name he thought I
         should take on as a disguise.

Goosh   The drama.

Sandy   Shut up, Goosh.

Johnny   Yes. Drama. Did you say your name is
         "Goosh?"

Goosh   Yeah. Why?

Johnny   It's a stupid name.

Goosh   Well, so is Johnny Ricotta.

Johnny   You're right. Regardless, I put my
          kids through college with that
          envelope money. And though I miss my
          father dearly, I'm grateful that Mr.
          Chalmers tried to look out for us.

Sandy   Well, I'm so sorry about your father.

Johnny   Thank you.

Goosh   And I'm sorry Chuy stole your name.

Johnny   Not at all. It's a good name. It was
          my father's name too. And I liked
          "Johnny." It's friendly. It's a
          little "wise-guy" but not too much. I
          didn't like Ricotta though. I felt
          like I'd need to name my son, Danny
          Parmesan or Mikey Mozzarella or
          somethin…

Goosh   Patty Pecorino.

Johnny   Right. Sorry I can't help with Mr.
          Chalmers' whereabouts. He was mixed
          up with some pretty dangerous fellas
          back when I knew him. I'd think most
          of those guys are old men themselves
          at this point. Either that or long-
          gone by now.

Sandy   Did he leave a clue or anything?

Johnny   What? No. I haven't seen him in 50
          years. I honestly wouldn't have
          thought he was still alive if the
          money hadn't kept showing up.

Sandy   Well I'm sorry if the money *quits*
        showing up. I didn't know anything
        about it and I've been keeping his
        books for the past 30 years.

Johnny No worries. We're well set up at this
        point. My mom passed away about 10
        years ago. My kids are out of school.
        They opened a restaurant in New York.
        My wife runs a yoga studio down the
        road. We're liquid on this building
        and the house. I only come in on
        Fridays so I can pick up the money
        and make some cuban sandwiches that
        people buy on DoorDash from my "ghost
        kitchen."[37]

[Johnny flips through the mail that's on the
counter]

        Well … whatdya know!

[He reveals an envelope addressed to "Johnny
Ricotta." Johnny opens the envelope to see
$1000 in cash and a letter.][38]

Goosh   It's a clue!

Mic   You love a treasure hunt don't you?

Goosh   We're trying to find our husband,
        Mic. And where's your sense of
        adventure?!

---

[37] The revealing of unnecessary information here is too much. It's just too much.

[38] This is rapidly becoming a children's detective story. My apologies.

Johnny, My Boy

I apologize, but this will be my last envelope. I've always thought of you as a son. I'm just kidding. Though I hope this finds you well.

If my husband and/or wife and/or a nice young ginger show up at your doorstep, they're not cops, they're not informants, they're family and I've gone missing. Please send them to Eddie's by the Lake. Yes ... it's still there. And let em take the bike. Tell em to live a little.

Peace and Love and Stars Above
If those bitches get nervous, give their asses a shove.

All the best,

Chuy

--

Goosh   Eddie's?

Johnny Yeah. Sounds like yall have your work
        cut out for you.

Mic   What's that supposed to mean?

Johnny He's got you on a treasure hunt.

Goosh   That's what I been sayin!

Johnny I don't really mean it in a good way.
        Have any of you been to Eddie's
        before?

Sandy   Oh, we've been to Eddie's plenty. You
        boys are on your own.

Goosh   What?! Why?

Sandy   I used to go with Eddie a lifetime
        ago. He was killed in a horrible drug
        raid in the 90s. I'll never go back.[39]

Goosh   We know. We know!

Mic   I *DON'T* know. But I *DO* know that I'm
        sitting this one out. I don't need to
        be treasure hunting at some bar by
        the lake because of some letter that
        was mailed to an old Cuban dude who
        runs a non-functioning Italian
        restaurant in an Irish neighborhood.

Johnny Sure ya do, buddy! That's the
        American dream!

---

[39] Again with the drama-club. The writing is so lazy.

[Johnny briskfully removes a dusty sheet to reveal a motorcycle with a side car.]

Sandy   Okay … I'm back in. Goosh, you're riding bitch. Mic, you're on the back.

Mic   No.

[Stage goes to black. Then the sound of sound of steel drum music, bar chatter, and motorcycles that we heard at the opening of the show returns.]

Eddie

[Lights come to reveal the "Go Shuck
 Yourself! I'm at Sandy's" sign again.
 Motorcycle enters with Sandy, Goosh, and
 Mic.]

Mic   You didn't tell me this place was in
          Sandusky. My ass is going to feel
          this tomorrow.

Goosh   That's what HE said.[40]

Sandy   Stop being a baby. Wait … This isn't
          Eddie's. [Sandy noticing the
          "Sandy's" sign]

          Mickey! Mickey! Get my picture. Sandy
          at Sandy's! Look at this.

Mic   What do you mean, "this isn't
          Eddie's?"

Sandy   I mean, look at it, dummy. Someone
          changed the name to *Sandy's*. It's me,
          Sandy. I'm at *Sandy's.*

Mic   Sure. But this *is* where we're
          supposed to be, right?

Goosh   Oh yeah … honestly, Mic, this place
          hasn't changed a bit. They literally
          just changed the signage. It smells
          the same and everything. And God!
          They still have the flamingos and the
          bubbles! Lord, what a mess.

---

[40] Sorry. Had to.

Sandy   Shut up, Goosh. It's great. This is like a time machine, Mickey. I haven't been here in ages. It brings up so many memories. But that life's behind me now. God … I need a drink.

[Eddie pops up from behind the bar]

Eddie   Sorry to keep you waiting. What can I get—

[Sandy and Eddie make eyes. Sandy screams and faints. Eddie, who looks like Chuy but with a ponytail and a bad goatee, jumps over the bar and lifts her head off the ground in the style of a Prince-Charming-type. Sandy wakes.][41]

Sandy   Eddie? How … I thought …

Eddie   Yes darling. It's me, Eddie. From before. You thought I was dead but I am alive. And I'm sorry I … I'm sorry I didn't let you know that I was still alive. That's … my bad. [Eddie and Sandy start making out sloppily.]

Mic   What the fuck is going on?

Sandy   But Eddie … I thought you were *dead*.[42]

---

[41] I must apologize. This sequence is the worst acting/writing up to this point. Eddie's a heavy-handed mess. I hope you can smell his ponytail. I hope you can hear is goatee. And Sandy … lord … Sandy's right there with him. They deserve each other. Really.

[42] So sorry.

Eddie   Yes my darling. We've covered that.
Anyways … friends, it is I, Eddie
Mercury. Almost dead, but very much
still alive, proprietor of "Sandy's"
formerly "Eddie's" at the Lake: Your
home for Local Craft Beers, Non-Local
Oysters, and the best live music
between Cleveland and Toledo. Goosh!
Great to see you my old friend. It's
been far too long.

Goosh   Eddie! Great to see you. You're
looking very … *alive* these days.
That's … great.

Mic   Did he say his name was "Eddie
Mercury?" [43]

Sandy   Eddie! I'm so glad to see you. But
we're looking for Chuy! He's gone
missing.

Eddie   Chuy Chalmers is missing?! Oh my!
What happened?

Sandy   We don't know Eddie. We're hoping you
could help us.

Eddie   Help *you?* Find *Chuy?* After he *set me
up!?* After he … left me for dead!?
After he stole the love of my life …
my … Sandy … from me. You want ME to
help YOU find HIM? [44]

---

[43] This is truly insane. And we're just not going to talk about it?

[44] Again … so sorry.

Goosh   [to Mic] This is so stupid.[45]

Mic   Yeah … it's a bit over the top

Goosh   Yeah. I'm kinda over it. But I really want that boat.

Mic   What?[46]

Goosh   I want the boat. Chuy's letter said if we find him, I get the boat. That's why I'm putting up with all this bullshit. I'm hoping when we get to the end of this little field trip and "find Chuy" or whatever that means, I end up with the boat, Sandy ends up with the house, and you can get your little book money or whatever you're doing here.

Mic   I honestly DON'T know what I'm doing here. But you *honestly* think we're going to "*find Chuy*" at the end of this?

Goosh   I suppose. But I imagine we have to wait for him to "reveal himself" or something.

Mic   Yeah … I didn't want to be "*THAT guy*" earlier but that Johnny-guy was definitely Chuy, right?

---

[45] Finally some acknowledgement.

[46] Goosh and Mic finally get into it here. But if you're wondering … Yes, of course … Eddie and Sandy are either 'making eyes' at each other during this dialogue or fully snogging. Whatever is funniest and what the actors are comfortable with.

Goosh   What? Oh … that guy back there at
          that "Italian" restaurant? Oh, for
          sure.

Mic   And *this guy* here…

Goosh   Eddie? *Yeah*. Eddie's *definitely* Chuy.
          But Eddie's a really good bass
          player. Chuy and I used to come to
          this bar all the time and Eddie had
          this awesome band that would only
          play Queen and Eddie Money songs.

Mic   Okay. And that's why he's called
          "Eddie Mercury?" [47]

Goose   Huh … Never really thought about it.

Mic   Goosh … What the fuck is this? You
          just said that Eddie *IS* Chuy then you
          IMMEDIATELY started talking about
          Eddie like he was another person!

Goosh   [ignoring Mic] Eddie … we need your
          help. We wouldn't ask for it if we
          didn't need it.[48]

Eddie   I told you … I want nothing to do
          with Chuy Chalmers. He set me up in
          that drug bust and I had to fake my
          own death and I lost my Sandy and
          that life is behind me now.

Sandy   I didn't know he set you up, Eddie. I
          swear.

---

[47] Seriously though … the dude is called, Eddie Mercury, and he plays Queen and
Eddie Money covers, exclusively? Are you not entertained?

[48] Okay … now I'm upset again.

Eddie   That life's behind me now. I don't want to talk about it, Sandy.

Mic   It kinda feels like you want to talk about it, Eddie.

Eddie   And who the fuck is this little nark?

Goosh   Woah! Easy big fella. This is Mic. He's writing a book about Chuy.

Eddie   Why would you want to write a story about that lying, stealing, sack of shit?

Mic   It's not that I *want* to. I've kinda been dragged into whatever THIS is.

Eddie   Well, I don't know *nothin about nothin.*

Mic   Yeah … The last guy said that too.

Eddie   Don't press me, young man. You don't wanna see the things I've seen.

Mic   You're probably right.

Sandy   Do it for me, Eddie. Help us. Chuy's gone. I'm back. You're back.

Goosh   We're so back.

Sandy   Help us Eddie.

Eddie   How do you want ME to help? I don't
        know where he is. I haven't thought
        about him in ages. It's not like I've
        spent hours every day thinking about
        how he stabbed me in the back with
        that drug run and left me for dead
        and stole my girl and took my whole
        life from me.

Mic   The "drug bust thing" is just *so
        vague.*

Goosh   I know, right? Like we need more
        details or something. You keep
        bringing it up then dropping it. Like
        … tell us more or don't. Ya know?

Eddie   *I'll never tell.*

Goosh   Fine. Ther. don't. I don't care. But
        stop bringing it up or we're gonna
        ask questions about it. Do you want
        us to ask about it?

Eddie   Don't even think about it.

Goosh   Fine. Sorry.

Eddie   It was 1992. Me and my tribe were
        moving a lot of … *packages* … for a …
        logistics company. Chuy was my
        contact. We'd done a lot of work
        together in the past. We were
        friends. I had no reason not to trust
        him. He had colleagues on the inside
        who'd assured us a safe passage from
        Atlanta to Detroit. We don't usually
        travel South to North. But the price
        was right.

Goosh   [to Mic] This is so dramatic.

Mic   [to Goosh] I know.

Eddie   We were so close. Maybe 40 miles
         south of Toledo and we ran into an
         ambush. The feds were everywhere. The
         few of us on enduros went into a
         patch of forest. We were ripping
         through the trees for 15 minutes or
         so. We could hear the helicopters
         circling the area. My Sargent put his
         bike against a log and flew off-
         empaling himself on a tree limb. I
         climbed that tree, switched vests
         with him, put my wallet his his
         pocket and took his for my own. They
         surrounded the area and found me. I
         told them that I was the Sargent and
         that the Sargent was 'Eddie.' They
         took me at my word. And just like
         that, Eddie Mercury was dead.

Goosh   Wow.[49]

Sandy   We thought you were gone, Eddie.

Eddie   Everyone did. I did 24 years in the
         state pen. The day I got out, I
         hitched a ride up here to see what
         was left of the old bar. It'd been
         bought by a girl who'd named the bar
         after her mother. A mother … she'd
         never had the *chance* to remember…[50]

Sandy   Oh Eddie. Where is she?

---

[49] "Wow" is right.

[50] Oh no…

Eddie   Oh … *OUR* daughter?...

Mic   Jesus Christ.

Eddie   Today's her day off.

Sandy   I'd really like to see her.

Goosh   Jesus Christ.

Eddie   I'll take you to her.

Sandy   I can't! We've got to find Chuy!

Eddie   I lost you once, Sandy. I'm not going
         to lose you again.

Mic   [to Goosh] It's too much.

Goosh   [to Mic] Yeah. It's just too much.

Sandy   Boys…

Goosh   [nonchalantly] Go … just go.

Mic   Yeah … we'll figure it out. I hate
         this.

Sandy   Thanks guys. If you do find Chuy …
         you tell him I love him.

Goosh   Okay. Whatever.

[Eddie and Sandy ride away on the motorcycle
 the gang rode from Johnny's in Cleveland]

[Goosh and Mic look at each other and
 realize *that* was their ride.]

Mic   I wish they wouldn't have taken *OUR*
         bike.

Goosh   Yeah … I don't know how we're getting
        home.

Mic   We've gotta talk.

Goosh   Whatever, Mic. We've gotta figure out
        how to get outta here.

Mic   So Johnny Ricotta and Eddie Mercury
        are both Chuy, right?

Goosh   I guess.

Mic   You guess?! What the fuck is that
        supposed to mean.

Goosh   I don't know.

Mic   You don't know WHAT? You don't know
        if those two dudes are just Chuy in
        bad costumes doing bad monologues or
        you don't know what I'm asking?

Goosh   What ARE you asking?

Mic   I'm asking you to tell me what the
        fuck is going on!

Goosh   You think I know? You think I
        wouldn't tell you if I knew? I don't
        fucking know. I live my life like
        this, Mic. I get dragged into shit
        like this all the time. This is just
        a Saturday for me, dude. My life is
        chaotic. We don't live under normal
        circumstances.

You normies out there in the normal world living your boring-ass lives make up stupid stories about other people all the time. You go on the internet and find some conspiracy theory abcut someone you don't know and combine it with another conspiracy theory about some place you'll never see.

You bicker back and forth and back and forth about politicians and celebrities and other boring ass people. Cus that's all you know. You're inventing ways to make boring-ass people a little bit more interestir.g. But it's all talk. It's all words. And it doesn't even have anything to do with YOUR LIFE. None of yall are really DOING anything. It's just commentary.

You ever think about it, Mickey? You ever think, "hmm … I wonder what life would be like if I decided it didn't need to be this fucking boring?"

What if you decided to go outside and do anything at all?

"What if I went on a hike? What if I went to the movies?"

That'd be *big* for you, right? If you decided to leave your house and go outside and see something other than whatever slop they put in front of you online. That'd be a big day for you, right?

That's nothin for me, Mic. My life is
full of people who've decided not to
consume ANYTHING. We're producers,
Mic. We're the makers! We're the ones
who season the slop.

There's two kinds of people in this
world, babe. Producers and Consumers.
That's it. And you know what yall's
problem is? You know what the problem
with this world is? It's that yall
are too scared to MAKE ANYTHING. You
just talk about things that already
exist. Even your art! God. It's all
politics. It's all commentary.
Aren't you people tired? Isn't it
exhausting to do nothing for no
reason? You really don't want to MAKE
anything? You don't want to BUILD
ANYTHING?! Hell … you don't even want
to eat anything that's any bit
spicy?! You're just eating overcooked
food and waiting to die? That's it?!
What a waste.

Not me, Mic. That ain't me.

That ain't me. That ain't Sandy. That
ain't Johnny. That ain't Eddie. And
that definitely isn't Chuy Chalmers.

[a man who's taken a seat at the bar chimes
 in]

Donnie Did you say "Chuy Chalmers?"

[Mic and Goosh turn]

Mic   Oh no.

Goosh   Donnie, baby! Is that you? Jesus!
It's been at least a few years.
Donnie, this is my dear friend, Mic
Fox.

Donnie   Oh … I know Mic Fox. How you been
man?

Mic   I'm good Donnie. I'm good.

[to audience]

Actually … I'm not good. Donnie's in this story now.
And we'll say that's … "upsetting" at best.

If you've read my book, you may remember Donnie.

He's a … let's call him a "creature" from the Lake Erie
Island community. "Creature" might be too generous.

He's a sex-pest. Yeah … That feels more honest.
I first observed Donnie in his natural habitat, floating
inside a metaphorical Long-Island Iced-Tea in a town
and/or state-of-mind called Put-In-Bay, Ohio. And like
I said, calling him a "bar-rat" is doing him a lot of
service. He's a serial predator and a grown-up Lost-Boy
from Peter Pan.

Last time I saw Donnie, he was smoking a cigarette and
running from a hearse that he'd purchased from a
defunct haunted-house-business. He was running from
said hearse because it was seconds away from being
engulfed in flames. If you'd like to hear the rest of
THAT story, you can purchase '*Midwestern Pulp*'
where ever books are sold.

Regardless … I am displeased to see Donnie. As I'm
certain that this is NOW either…

A: a bad dream; or

        B: my life is about to become more "exciting" but in a bad way.

Donnie   Goosh … you know Mickey here wrote a book about me…

Goosh   I DID know that, Donnie. That's actually how Mic and I met. See, Chuy's having Mickey write a book about him too.

Donnie   Well aint that something.

Mic   Donnie, you're looking … well.[51]

Donnie   Thank you, my good man. This is a new jacket.

Mic   That can't be true.

Goosh   Donnie! Maybe you could be of some help to us.

Mic   Here we go.

Goosh   Chuy's gone missing, Donnie.

Donnie   Chuy's gone missing?!

["BomBomBom" music hits. Donnie and Goosh turn to the audience.]

Mic   Yeah … anyway … Donnie, Chuy is missing and we're on a wild-goose-chase at this point.

---

[51] He's obviously not. Dude is a slime-ball. He's wearing his trademark fur-coat with no shirt underneath and some very long jorts (jean-shorts).

Donnie   More of a wild "GOOSH-chase" if you
          ask me.

Goosh   [flirty] Donnie! Staaaahp…"

Mic   He left us some clues and wants us to
          come find him or something. He ran us
          to this weird Italian restaurant and
          to THIS strange-ass bar and now we're
          talking to you, which is obviously
          upsetting.

          So if you have some fucked up riddle
          or something you need to share,
          please get on with it. As I and
          [gesturing to the crowd] these lovely
          people need to get home and process
          our life choices.

Donnie   Relax, Mic. All will be revealed in
          time. But here's a place to start…

[music begins. Goosh and Donnie arrange
 themselves as if they're about to begin a
 musical number.][52]

Mic   Absolutely not! I told them earlier.
          We're not doing any sort of musical
          number. Absolutely not. Stop it.
          Stop. Now. No. Fuck you, Donnie!

Donnie   He's such a fucking square.

Goosh   I know. So young. So jaded.

Donnie   No fun. All business.

---

[52] Oh my…I thought I had this under control. I swear. But Donnie's here now. So I
guess we're fully off the rails here. So sorry.

Goosh   [mocking Mic's voice] "Howdy Howdy …
        you boys better get to the point."

Donnie "Pipe down back there. We've got a
        missing person on our hands."

Goosh   "Yeah … where in the world *IS* Carmen
        SanDiego?"

Donnie Relax Mickey. We'll find Chuy. But a
        guy like Chuy only gets found when he
        wants to be.

Mic   I'm coming to terms with that. Have
        you seen him recently?

Goosh   [to Donnie] He's sooo "detective"
        isn't he?

Donnie [laughing] Yeah … I think that Carmen
        SanDiego comment cut him to his core.

Mic   Donnie … Do you know where he is?

Donnie I don't. I'm sorry. I honestly
        haven't seen him in years.

Mic   Then what the hell was the musical
        number going to be about?

Donnie I don't know. It just felt like
        that's where things were going?
        Right, Goosh?

Goosh   Oh for sure … the music started up
        and everything.

Donnie Exactly. I'm just going with the
        flow.

Mic   You gotta have something for us,
         Donnie. Please. I'm so tired.

Donnie   I'm serious. I've got nothin. I
         haven't seen him since Chandler's
         funeral.

Mic   Who is Chandler?

Donnie   What's up?

Mic   Who is Chandler? You just said, "I
         haven't seen Chuy since Chandler's
         funeral."

Donnie   Oh yeah! Chandler is Chuy's brother.
         He passed away a few years ago.
         That's the last time I saw Chuy too.
         He was pretty tore up about it. Goosh
         and Chuy picked me up in this awesome
         old tugboat on the way to the
         funeral. You guys still have that
         boat?

Goosh   You know it.

Donnie   That thing is sweet. You should see
         it Mickey.

Mic   Oh … I've seen the boat. Please
         continue.

Donnie   Continue what?

Mic   For the love of God … you've gotta
         have more than that.

Donnie   More what?

Mic   You've gotta have something! You know
        SOMETHING DONNIE! CHRIST! You've
        gotta know something!

Donnie Chill dude! This is a new jacket. Did
        you reach out to his brother?

Mic   What are you talking about?

Donnie Did you call Chuy's brother and see
        if he knows where Chuy is?

Mic   You literally JUST SAID his brother
        died, Donnie.

Donnie Not Chandler, Mic. He's dead. Chuck.
        Goosh … you called Chuck already,
        right?

Goosh   Chuck doesn't have service out there,
        Donnie. And shit … I haven't seen
        Chuck since the funeral, either.

Donnie I mean … if I'm Chuy, and I'm hiding
        out from something … West Sister is
        where I'd go.

Goosh   No way. He's not "hiding out" from
        something. He WANTS us to find him.
        Chuy wants Mic to compile all these
        stories from "people in his past" and
        turn it into a book. And he said if
        we find him, I get the boat.

Donnie   Ha! And you think he's gonna make it
         easy for you to find him then? Yeah
         right! Chuy's a monster. And a liar.
         I bet he's made this seem like a
         funny little treasure hunt. But he's
         hiding something. And if he's hiding
         from something, I bet his ass is out
         on that scary little island. He knows
         you'd never put the effort in to come
         find him out there. And even if you
         did make it … you still might not
         find him.

Goosh   You really think he's out there?

Donnie   I mean … it's a hike. But if I'm a
         monster who's looking to stay lost …
         that's where I'd go.

Mic   How far out are we talkin?

Donnie   That's the spirit, Mickey!

Goosh   How far is it, Donnie?

Donnie   Man … I don't know … 15 miles maybe.

Mic   That's not *that* far.

Donnie   Sure. Not on land. But we've gotta
         get to the other side of the islands.
         If we're bookin it … it'll take an
         hour or so.

Mic   Where are we talkin?

Donnie   West Sister.

Goosh   West Sister? I hardly know her.

Donnie   That was nice, Goosh! [high-fiving]

Mic   What's that?

Donnie   West Sister Island. It's west of the
         big islands. Kinda out there on its
         own. I think it's a nature reserve or
         somethin now. But Chuck's been fixin
         up the old lighthouse quarters for a
         few years. And they let him stay out
         there.

Mic   So what's on the island.

Goosh   Poison Ivy mostly.

Donnie   I mean … yeah … that's about it. I
         think it's closed to the public. No
         ferry or nothin. Just Chuck and the
         lighthouse and a buncha snakes and
         shit. Maybe some bodies. I don't
         know. It sucks.

Goosh   It's the worst, Mic. I'd rather not.

Mic   Yeah … I don't need to go out there.

Donnie   I mean … it's definitely not worth
         it. But if yall have money in this or
         if you're trying to write a book
         about Chuy, Chuck's a guy you've
         gotta talk to.

Mic   I don't think I'm up for it, guys. I
         don't know what's real anymore. We
         just spent the day talking to people
         that may or may not exist. And I'm
         tired. I'm confused. I'm hungry.

Donnie   They've actually got really good food
         here, dude.

Goosh   Yeah. Eddie's brother, Teddy make's a
         mean little smash burger.

Mic   I don't care! I don't know if Eddie
         is real or if Chuy's real. Shit … I
         don't know if *you're real*, Donnie!
         And we've fucking met before! I don't
         know what the hell this is.

Donnie   This is as real as anything else,
         Mickey. We're all making it up as we
         go. Finish the story, babe. Live a
         little.

[cut to black.]

[Video montage of Donnie, Goosh, and Mic on
 a single jetski cut with a map of them
 traveling to West Sister Island, OH]

Chuck Chalmers

[The gang gets to the island, asses sore.]

Goosh   An hour on a jetski is a fucking
         nightmare. My ass is going to feel
         this tomorrow.

Donnie   That's what she said.[53]

Goosh   Nice. [high-fiving]

Mic   This is no good.[54]

Donnie   Whatchu mean?

Mic   I have a horrible feeling about this.

Donnie   Why?

Mic   Why do you think? Look at this place.
         It's a decrepit old lighthouse in the
         middle of Lake Erie on an island that
         I've never heard of in my life that's
         literally covered in poison ivy. This
         is no good.

Goosh   Yeah. This is why we don't come up
         here. And Chuck's a fucking weirdo.

Mic   THANK YOU FOR REVEALING THIS NOW,
         GOOSH.

---

[53] So sorry.

[54] West Sister Island is 82 acres of Hackberry trees and Poison Ivy. It's completely closed to the public and is the home to a buncha birds and Chuy's brother, Chuck, I guess.

Goosh   What? You didn't think Chuy's *last
        remaining identical brother that
        lives in a dilapidated lighthouse on
        an island that's covered in poison
        ivy was gonna be a weirdo?*

Mic   WHAT?!

Goosh   What? Is that so alarming to you?

Mic   We're meeting Chuy's twin brother?

Goosh   Well … I guess they're twins *NOW*.

Mic   What the fuck is that supposed to
        mean?

Goosh   They *WERE* triplets.

Donnie They're still triplets, Goosh. Just
        because Chandler died doesn't mean
        Chuck and Chuy are twins now.

Mic   So, you're telling me that Chuy has
        two identical brothers named Chandler
        and Chuck. Chandler is dead and we're
        about to meet Chuck who lives in a
        lighthouse in the middle of nowhere?

Goosh   I think you got it.

Donnie Yeah. That's right.

Goosh   Why?

Mic   No reason. I'm just adding this to a
        list of ridiculous nonsense that I've
        heard today.

Goosh   Okay, chill.

[Donnie, Mic, and Goosh approach the door of the lighthouse]

Donnie   Alrighty, guys. It's been real. I'll wait out here for you.

Mic   Nah. Your ass is definitely coming with us.

Donnie   Oh … I'd like to. But Chuck told me at Chandler's funeral that he'd kill me if he ever saw me again.

Mic   That's upsetting.

Goosh   Oh yeah! That's right!

Mic   What happened?

Donnie   Well Mic, you'll actually get a kick out of this. You know that old hearse I used to drive around that exploded up at Put-In-Bay?[55]

Mic   I do.

Donnie   Chandler was helping me move it onto the ferry so we could take it to salvage back at Port Clinton. But the parking break failed as we were loading it and the car smashed his leg.

Mic   Jesus.

Donnie   Yeah. And he was bleeding so bad. They had to life-flight his ass to Toledo.

---

[55] Again … another story for another time.

Mic   And that's how he died?!

Donnie   No. But they did have to amputate his
          leg.

Mic   Jesus Christ!

Donnie   Yeah. And he was doin pretty good. I
          came over a couple days after his
          surgery to bring him some flowers.

Goosh   Chandler *loved* flowers. He was the
          florist for Princess Diana's
          funeral.[56]

Donnie   That's right. I went to go bring him
          some flowers. And then my fucking
          dog, bit his other leg. And it got
          all infected...

Mic   And *that's how he died?!*

Donnie   No no. He was in the hospital for a
          week or so. They had to amputate that
          leg too. But while he was in the
          hospital I built him this ramp so he
          could get in and out of the house and
          I guess the ramp was too steep or
          somethin and he rolled down the ramp
          and down the driveway and into the
          road and he got hit by some dude in a
          truck who was driving home from Bash
          On The Bay.[57]

---

[56] There's no way this is true.

[57] 'Bash On The Bay' is a wild-ass concert they throw every summer up at Put-In-Bay. Also, Put-In-Bay, OH is a real place. Imagine Ohio's take on the Florida Keys.

Goosh   Who played that year?

Donnie I think this was 2021 … so maybe …
        Brad Paisley or somethin.

Goosh   No. That was the year after. Cus they
        did a tribute for Chandler, right?

Donnie That's right! Who was the year
        before?

Goosh   Blake Shelton!

Donnie That's right. Blake and Shelton and
        Keith Urban. Love me some Keith
        Urban. He's got great hair.[58]

Mic   What the fuck is wrong with you
        people?

Goosh   What?

Mic   You hit this man with your car then
        he got bit by your dog then he got
        hit by another car and that's how he
        died?!

Donnie Yep. That's how he died. He got hit
        by that truck. And Chuck got so bent
        out of shape about it. I remember
        what he said. He said, "If I ever see
        you or anyone you love ever again,
        I'm going to kill you, process your
        remains into sausages, and put those
        sausages in my freezer."[59]

---

[58] This is so twisted.

[59] Woah! Not chill. Too specific.

Goosh   Drama!

Mic   And *that's* who we're going to talk to
         right now?

Donnie   That's who YOU're going to talk to
         right now. I'm no sausage. I'll wait
         down by the jetski.

[Goosh knocks on the door. The door opens on
 its own.]

Mic   Absolutely not.

Goosh   What?

Mic   What do you mean what?

Goosh   We're already here. He's my missing
         husband's identical twin brother. I
         haven't seen him in years. He's not
         that crazy. He's just kind of a
         grump.

Mic   The kind of grump who doesn't want to
         be bothered to the point where he
         lives in a lighthouse on an
         uninhabited island?

Goosh   I mean … when you put it like that…

[Goosh and Mic enter the lighthouse. It's as
 eerie as you'd expect.]

Mic   I can't. We gotta get outta here.

Goosh   HEY CHUCK! It's Goosh! Are you here?

Chuck   [from off stage] Hello?

Goosh   CHUCK! It's Goosh! Chuy's roommate!

98

Mic   [to Goosh] Chuy's *"Roommate?"*

Goosh   [to Mic] Chuck's kind of a homophobe.
           Be cool.

Mic   Jesus.

[Chuck reveals himself. He looks exactly
 like Chuy but he's got on an old lighthouse
 keepers hat.][60]

Chuck   Goosh! Is that really you? How are
           you my friend? It's been too long!

Goosh   It truly has been.

Chuck   I'm glad you announced yourself. I
           don't get many visitors. And of those
           visitors, very few of them AREN'T
           greeted with my ol *Smith and Wesson.*

[silence then Chuck laughs chaotically then
 Goosh and Mic laugh nervously]

Chuck   I kid. Who's your friend Goosh? Some
           strange tail yall picked up at the
           Bass Pro Shop, I imagine. I kid. I
           kid.

Goosh   This is our good friend, Mic Fox,
           Chuck.

Chuck   I know *that* name … is this the lad
           who wrote that book you sent me?

Goosh   It is.

---

[60] This is alarming to say the least. I'm officially stressed out at this point.

Chuck   I loved it, Mic! Hilarious. And based on your writing, it sounds like you met our friend, *Donnie* … I'm sorry to hear that.

Mic   Me too.

[Chuck laughs maniacally]

Chuck   He's a stupid son of a bitch. And he did kill our brother. But he means well. I'll kill him if I ever see him again. But he means well. [laughs again]

    To what do I owe this surprise drop-in, boys? Can I get you something to drink?

Goosh   I'd love something.

Mic   I'm okay.

Chuck   Live a little, Mickey.

[Chuck hand them each a drink. The three of them sit. Mic, hesitantly]

Goosh   I'm afraid we've got a situation on our hands, Chuck.

Chuck   Well, you've come to the right place. See Mickey, I'm the guy people come to when they need a "situation" "handled."

Goosh   Well … Chuy is missing.

Chuck   Okay … on purpose or is he missing
        missing?[61]

Goosh   The former, I believe.

Chuck   Ah … He does this on occasion. It's
        been a while though. Why's he gone
        missing?

Goosh   Well, he approached, Mr. Fox here to
        see about helping him ghost-write his
        memoirs.

Chuck   I see!

Goosh   You do?

Chuck   Yes. He wants to write this book but
        he needs help because he can't read
        or write?

Goosh   That's how it started.

Chuck   But you know he *can* read and write,
        right?

Goosh   Right.

Chuck   And you know he's like … a liar,
        right? Like … his whole life story is
        fictionalized?

Goosh   Sure. We're not sure to what extent
        we're sure. But we sorta-understand
        what he's cookin.

Mic   Do we?

---

[61] Well … he handled that calmly.

Chuck   You talk to anyone else about this?

Goosh   In a way.

Chuck   What the fuck's that supposed to mean?[62]

Goosh   Easy. I mean … Chuy left some clues.

Chuck   Okay. Who'd you talk to?

Goosh   We met a man on the Westside of Cleveland who runs a little Italian restaurant.

Chuck   Which restaurant?

Goosh   I don't actually know what it's called.

Mic   We met a guy called, Johnny.

Chuck   AH! Johnny Ricotta!

Goosh   That's the one.

Chuck   He's a good one. I like that guy. He's Puerto Rican or something, right?

Mic   Cuban.

Chuck   That's right. Good sandwiches. Anyone else?

Goosh   There was a clue at Johnny's that sent us to Eddie's.

---

[62] Uh-Oh. Don't love *that* tone shift.

Chuck   Very nice! How's Eddie? They thought he was dead for a while, you know?

Goosh   Yep. That's right. He's not dead though.

Chuck   Oh that's great. Was Sandy with yall?

Mic   She was.

Chuck   And she got to see Eddie?

Goosh   She did.

Chuck   Oh that's great! I bet she lost her mind! Did she know he was still alive?

Goosh   Seemingly not.

Chuck   That's great!

Goosh   They ran off together.

Chuck   Who?

Mic   Sandy and Eddie.

Chuck   No way! They were old sweethearts, Mic. They go way back.

Mic   So I've been told.

Chuck   Anyone else?

Goosh   Well…

Chuck   What?

Mic   [to Goosh] Just tell him…

Chuck   What?

Goosh   … well …

Chuck   [getting heated and standing up]
           You fucking tell me who else you
           talked to right now.

Mic   We ran into Donnie.

Chuck   What?

Goosh   Donnie was at Eddie's. We assumed he
           had the next clue. He told us to come
           talk to you.

Chuck   About what?

Mic   About Chuy.

Chuck   What about him?

Goosh   Do you know where he is?

Chuck   Where Chuy is?

Mic   Yes!

Chuck   No.

Goosh   No, what?!

Chuck   No. I don't know where Chuy is. Is
           Donnie here right now?

[Mic and Goosh look at each other]

Goosh   He dropped us off.

Chuck   Okay. So how are you boys gonna get
           off this island.

Goosh   We're not 100% sure yet.

Mic   Yeah. We haven't had much of a plan today, honestly. We just keep taking strange forms of transportation to strange places. I was hoping you had some story about Chuy that would lead us to another form of strange transportation that would get us closer to finding Chuy.

Chuck   Well … I hate to disappoint you boys, but I haven't seen Chuy in a couple months. We got lunch at Eddie's at the beginning of the summer. But he didn't mention anything about no memoir or anything like that. He did mention something about "shaking things up." He seemed kinda slower than usual. I don't know how long you've known him, Mic, but he's usually quite chipper.

Goosh   What do you think he meant by, "shaking things up?"

Chuck   I don't know.

       [Chuck pauses then picks back up but slower.]

       He seemed sad.

       He seemed slower.

       He said he was feeling like he wasn't able to keep up with his bullshit anymore. Like he wasn't in control of his life. Like he didn't know what was real and what wasn't.

He said he was starting to feel the seasons change.

He said he felt himself getting old.

He started to forget...

[long pause]

He said he didn't want to be Chuy anymore.

He said ... [Chuck gets choked up]

[silence.] [63]

---

[63] Goosh and I realize we're talking to Chuy at this point. But Chuy's tired of being Chuy right now. And he's in a delicate spot. A spot no man ever prepares themselves to be in. Forgetting is humbling. Forgetting is isolating.

Humans are delicate creatures. Society pretends that they're not. But they are. They're expected to maintain control, peace, and structure but without any support system. Their problems are theirs alone. To seek help is weakness. Quietness is strength.

The narrative that society puts on us is not based on or to the benefit of the human experience. It's based purely upon the narratives of the past – narratives that DON'T even accurately reflect the past. Fantasies. Fantasies of a past where people *didn't have problems like these.*

To ignore the problems of today while fantasizing about the lack-of-problemed-past gets us nowhere. It keeps us CONSUMING nostalgia-flavored vitamins and cure-all-based supplements while we put off our problems, alone.

The only way out of this cycle is community. Real community. Acknowledge the problems, together. Relish in the time between. Don't go at the problems alone. And don't hoard all the wealth for yourself. Don't scapegoat your problems. Face them with grace and acceptance. Share the bounty. Tackle the problems, together. And create a narrative your community can believe in rather than consuming the system's newest scapegoat.

Goosh   It's okay, Chuck.

Mic   Yeah. It's okay … It's okay to feel
         out of control. No one's *really* in
         control of their life. We're just
         kinda … surfing the waves that come
         our way.

[silence]

Mic   [breaking silence, slowly and softly]
         So, Chuck … Chuy reached out to me to
         help him write his memoirs. And
         honestly … memoirs are kind of funny.
         Because they're based on memories.
         And memories are really just stories.
         And stories are just *that*. They're
         stories. They're lore.

         And lore's good. But life isn't all
         about the lore. It's about taking a
         breath every once in a while to relax
         with the people you love. It's about
         riding the waves.

And for the love of God, don't become stagnant and bitter and justify it by telling
yourself you're "conservative" or into "traditional values."

Traditional values are a farce. Because tradition is just a story. And those stories are
just fantasies of the past. They're stories. And you can't base the present or the future
on fantasies of the past. It's pretend. There's nothing *wrong* with playing pretend.
But don't drag everyone else into it, like a 7yr old at a dinner party.

The past is behind us. Go forward in love, peace, and acceptance. Bring people in.
Accept people for who they are and celebrate them. Celebrate them for their
differences and empower them to make the beautiful new future. Have nuance. And
please spend more time laughing and dancing. It's the only way up.

Wow … that one got away from me.

The waves aren't always at their breaking point. Sometimes the lake is glassy. Sometimes it's calm. And that's okay too.

Life isn't just the crazy stories. It isn't just your wildest memories. It's the time between the stories. It's the time between the waves.

And lord knows … I've been guilty of chasing the big waves … But I realize that a lot of the big waves aren't the best waves … at least not all the time. A lot of the best waves are *between* the big ones. They're the waves we get to surf together. That's where all the color comes from. That's where the big laughs are. That's the good stuff.

When I first met Chuy and Goosh and Sandy and Lil Ms. Dog, I was taken aback. Not by the lavishness, not by the lore, but by the way they were together. The way they finished each other's sentences. The way they gassed each other up. The way they laughed. Not the boat. Not the house. Not the tales of mobsters and motorcycle gangs or whatever the hell this is.

Being around them was enough. It's infectious. It's the little stuff. It's the ball busting. That's real love. That's where the life's at. *That's* why I agreed to write about this.

And sure, if I lived my life with the level of day-to-day wildness that I've experienced today, I'd probably have a hard time keeping up too. But you can enjoy surfing the smaller waves too. The time between the waves is what makes the waves … *the waves*. If the water's always high, there's no waves at all. It's just high tide.

[silence]

Goosh   Chuck … if you talk to Chuy…

[Goosh gets choked up.]

If you talk to Chuy could you tell him that his family misses him and cares about him and wants him to come home. We can find a way to shake things up if that's what he needs. We can find a way to make every day exciting … the way he's made it for us. We need him. He makes the times between the stories exciting. We need him between the waves.

[long silence. Chuck is thinking. He loses his train of thought. More silence]

Mic   Hey Chuck…

Chuck   Yeah?

Mic   Could you tell us a story about Chuy?

[the door opens]

Chuck   Well, speak of the devil … [points to the door] why don't you ask him yourself!

[Goosh and Mic turn to look at the door.]

[Cut to black.]

www.ingramcontent.com/pod-product-compliance
Lightning Source LLC
Chambersburg PA
CBHW021242090426
42740CB00006B/648